Friends With God

Drawings by Barbara Cooney

Friends With God

CATHERINE MARSHALL

STORIES AND PRAYERS
OF THE MARSHALL FAMILY

 AVON
PUBLISHERS OF BARD, CAMELOT AND DISCUS BOOKS

AVON BOOKS
A division of
The Hearst Corporation
959 Eighth Avenue
New York, New York 10019

First Avon Printing, January, 1973
Seventh Printing

AVON TRADEMARK REG. U.S. PAT. OFF. AND
FOREIGN COUNTRIES, REGISTERED TRADEMARK—
MARCA REGISTRADA, HECHO EN CHICAGO, U.S.A.

Printed in the U.S. A.

To Lynn and Bobby

The author wishes to express her appreciation to the Estate of Heywood Hale Broun and to Doubleday & Company, Inc., for permission to use "The Toy Dog," adapted from "Frankincense and Myrrh," reprinted by permission of the copyright owners; for "Bradley Keeps Books," adapted from CHILDREN'S STORY SERMONS by Hugh T. Kerr, published by the Fleming H. Revell Company; for "The Latchstring Was Out," adapted from THE FRIENDLY STORY CARAVAN, collected by a Committee of the Philadelphia Yearly Meeting of Friends, Anna Pettit Broomell, Chairman, Copyright 1935, 1948, 1949 by Anna Pettit Broomell, published by J. B. Lippincott Company, used by permission; for "Buying His Own," adapted from "The Story of the Lost Sail Boat," by Jacob J. Sessler, from JUNIOR SERMON STORIES, published by Fleming H. Revell Company; to Elizabeth Anne Campagna for permission to print her "I Knew God Was There"; to Mr. Joseph Allen for his invaluable help in research work in the Library of Congress; to my secretary, Margaret Bradley Giles, for her steady support and help. "There Is Gladness Everywhere," by Margaret E. Sangster was published by Harper & Brothers; "Solomon and the Bees" is based on an old legend taken from the Midrash; "The Easter Flower" is based on an Oriental legend; "Big Shot—the Little Sunfish," is an adaptation of a story by Worthington Stewart.

If there should remain any unacknowledged material in this book, the publisher will welcome word to that effect and will give proper credit in all future editions.

JESUS IS OUR FRIEND

We like to share happy times in our home with our friends. One day a group of Peter John's friends were playing Pirate Treasure Hunt. This was an exciting game. But it was a hard game for Tim, who was only four. Tim said, "My Friend Jesus will help me find the treasure."

Tim's older brother, David, was scornful. "That's a silly thing to say, Tim. You don't talk about the Lord Jesus that way. You just pray about important things, not everyday things."

After the game was finished, the children were sitting in front of the open fire looking at their treasures. David laughingly told of Tim's talking to his Friend Jesus about the Treasure Hunt.

I said, "I know what you mean, David. But Tim's feeling is right, you know.

Jesus does want to be our Friend. He told us so Himself."

"He did! Where?"

"Right in the fifteenth chapter of John. He really said it clearly, HENCEFORTH I CALL YOU NOT SERVANTS . . . BUT I HAVE CALLED YOU FRIENDS. . . . You know how we like to be with our friends often. Well, Jesus wants to be our Friend every day, not just on Sundays. And that, I think, is what Tim had in mind. He was certain that the Lord Jesus was here today with us in our fun."

After that, David and Peter John and the other children had so many adventures in learning to be God's friends, that they suggested that I tell you about some of them. That is why I decided to make this book. I hope that you too will decide that you want the fun of being FRIENDS WITH GOD.

Catherine Marshall

CONTENTS

FRIENDS WITH GOD

LITTLE DOG FOUND

Thank You, Jesus—Jeffey's home
again...
He woke me up this morning
scratching on the front door;
He was so tired and hungry
with what tail he has between his legs.
I think he'd like to say he's sorry ...
It's true, he's been a bad dog lately,
chewing up newspapers and jumping on
furniture;
But sometimes I've been bad too
and still You love me just the same ...
So, dear Jesus, will You love Jeff into
being good and help him not to run away
again? Thank you.

                                        Amen

THE EASTER FLOWER

When Jesus was a baby, His Mother Mary had to flee with Him to keep Him from being killed by the cruel King Herod. Joseph and Mary and the Baby crossed the hot plains of Jericho.

When Mary alighted from the ass on which she was riding, a little flower sprang up at her feet. It was as if the little flower wanted to greet the infant Saviour whom she carried in her arms.

These little yellow flowers sprang up at all the places where the Baby Jesus rested. And as He grew up, wherever He ran and played, there were the little flowers. He called them "Roses of Jericho."

Then came that sad day when He died on the cross. On that day all the little flowers withered and faded. But three days later, Jesus walked out of the tomb in which His friends had gently laid Him —alive forevermore. And as He walked out into the rose-tinted sunrise of that first Easter morning, the little Rose of Jericho sprang to life to greet Him. The little flowers began blooming gaily all over the land as a symbol of the joy in the earth, because Christ was risen.

That is why all of us are so happy at Easter. Flowers bloom in the fields and in our gardens just as did the Roses of Jericho. Some of the trees burst into

bloom. Birds joyously build their nests. Little girls wear flowers on their hats. Children dye eggs bright colors and laugh and sing. They are happy, not just because spring has come, but because they have a living Saviour to love. They know that Jesus will always be with them, to be their Friend and to help them.

Dear God:
Baby is too small to pray
Or thank You in a proper way;
Please bless her pudding and her meat
And everything she tries to eat.

Amen

Be our Guest, Lord Jesus,
At this festive board;
Give us joy in eating;
Be our Guest adored.

Amen

BUYING HIS OWN

With his father's help, a boy built a model motorboat with a real gasoline engine. The boy was very much excited when he took the boat for its trial run. He sailed it for some time on the river that ran near his house. But then, half-way across the stream, the motor stopped, and the little boat was carried downstream.

The boy tried hard to reach his boat, but could not. At last he had to go home without it. To him the boat was lost.

Not long afterward he and his father went to a nearby town farther down the river. In a shop window, the boy was surprised to see a model motorboat. A

sign on it read: THIS BOAT FOR SALE.
PRICE TWO DOLLARS.

But the boy knew that the boat was
the one he had lost. It was *his* boat!

He pulled his father into the shop. "I
made that boat," he told the storekeeper.
"See that red line of paint on the back
and the little scratch on the side. It's
mine. I lost it on the river."

But the storekeeper would not give it to him. "You can have it for two dollars," he said firmly.

Finally the father answered, "All right, son. We'll buy the boat back."

When the storekeeper took it from the window, the boy hugged the boat and said, "You are twice mine; I made you, and then I bought you back."

Of course the boat really belonged to the boy. And you see, we belong to God in just the same way. We are His because He made us. Then we are His, too, because He bought us back by sending His Son Jesus into our world to take us by the hand and lead us, each one, back to our Father.

TONGUES AND TOOTHPASTE

Tommy had been telling his playmates that Jim—the new boy—had cheated in the neighborhood baseball game. Tommy's father heard the story. Since he had seen the game, he doubted that Jim had cheated.

That night he and Tommy had a man-to-man talk about it. But Tommy didn't seem a bit troubled. He said, "O.K., maybe he didn't cheat. I'll just take back what I said."

"Will you?" his father answered. "You know, son, it isn't as easy as that. Come here with me." And he took Tommy into the bathroom.

There he handed Tommy a fat tube

of toothpaste. "Squeeze some out on the basin for me."

Tommy thought that was a queer thing to do. But he squeezed some of the toothpaste out onto the basin in long ribbon-like strips.

"Now, son—put that toothpaste back into the tube."

The little boy obediently tried. First he used the end of his toothbrush; then he tried a toothpick; then, his mother's nail file. But he soon found that there isn't any way to get toothpaste back into a tube.

"You see, Tommy," his father explained. "Your tongue let out a story that wasn't true. And you don't know how many people have heard that story

by now. You can't take your words back any more than you can put the toothpaste back."

Tommy hung his head. "Then how can I make it right for Jim?"

"You can't completely undo what you've done. But you can tell God you're sorry, and then ask Jim to forgive you."

"All right," said Tommy, thoughtfully. "But I guess it's really better not to squeeze the tube in the first place."

THERE IS GLADNESS EVERYWHERE

The ships glide in at the harbor's mouth,
And the ships sail out to sea,

And the wind that sweeps from the
sunny south
Is sweet as sweet can be.
There's a world of toil and a world of
pains,
And a world of trouble and care,

But O in a world where our Father
reigns,
There is gladness everywhere!
The harvest waves in the breezy morn,
And the men go forth to reap;
The fullness comes to the tasseled corn,

Whether we wake or sleep.
And far on the hills by feet untrod
There are blossoms that scent the air,
For O in this world of our Father, God,
There is beauty everywhere!
                —MARGARET ELIZABETH SANGSTER

BIG SHOT—
THE LITTLE SUNFISH

A fisherman had placed in a deep dishpan of water some fish he had caught in the lake. In the cottage by the side of the lake he began to clean the fish for the frying pan.

One by one he took out the fish and cut them up. And surely you will agree that things looked hopeless for the remaining fish in the dishpan.

But there was one little fish that had not given up hope. He was determined to get back to the lake. Of course, he didn't know where the lake was, but the first thing to do was to get out of the dishpan. So he jumped out.

As he flopped around on the floor, the fisherman scooped him up and put him back in the dishpan—and again he jumped out.

The fisherman was annoyed as he tossed him back again, but he was forced to notice this peppy little fellow who was so different from the others.

Next time the fisherman's hand was dipped into the dishpan for a fish the plucky one dodged out of reach and escaped. Then he hopped out again.

There was a bucket nearby, a bucket with high walls; so the fisherman dumped the whole mess into it and continued his job. But still, each time the fisherman groped in the bucket, the little fish escaped.

As the number of fish in the tub got down to a half dozen, this fish looked at the high walls of his prison and felt desperate. Worth trying, he thought. Why not? He gathered his strength. . . . Out he went.

This, the fisherman decided, would be a good time to clean him. But he just didn't have the heart.

"Get back in there, Big Shot," said the fisherman, and flipped him in.

One by one, the other fish were taken from the dishpan and cut up. Five, four, three, two—now only Big Shot and one dead companion remained. The little sunfish still didn't give up.

He flitted back and forth and round

and round. As his enemy watched, he nosed up and over the side of the bucket with startling suddenness.

The fisherman watched him for a moment. Then he dumped the dead fish into the garbage, ran some clean water from the faucet into the bucket, and put the fighting sunfish back in.

He picked up the bucket and walked down to the lake and dropped the little fish into the water. As the fisherman watched the small sunfish disappear into deep water with a final flip of his tail, he pondered a lesson he had just learned.

We are never licked until we quit.

Next time you are discouraged, think of Big Shot, the little sunfish!

WE THANK THEE

For flowers that bloom about our feet;
For tender grass, so fresh, so sweet;
For song of bird, and hum of bee;
For all things fair we hear or see,
   Father in heaven, we thank Thee!
For blue of stream and blue of sky;
For pleasant shade of branches high;
For fragrant air and cooling breeze;
For beauty of the blooming trees,
   Father in heaven, we thank Thee!
           —RALPH WALDO EMERSON

BRADLEY KEEPS BOOKS

Bradley was a little boy who had begun to think that money could buy anything. He had never stopped to think that gold cannot buy the most important thing in the world—Love.

One morning when Bradley came down to breakfast he put on his mother's plate a little piece of paper neatly folded. His mother opened it. She could hardly believe it, but this is what Bradley had written:

going to store _____ 25¢
dumping trash _____ 10¢
taking old musik
            leson — 15¢
Hanging up things 05¢
total _____ 55¢

His mother smiled but did not say anything. When lunchtime came she placed the bill on Bradley's plate with fifty-five cents.

Bradley's eyes fairly danced when he saw the money. "Boy, I'm in business," he said. But with the money there was another little bill which read like this:

Bradley owes Mother and Dad

For being good ——————— 00¢
For clothes, shoes and
            playthings — 00¢
For meals and his beautiful
           room — 00¢
For nursing him through
    his long illness with
    scarlet fever ——— 00¢

Total Bradley owes Mother and Dad — 00¢

Tears came into Bradley's eyes. He put his arms around his mother's neck, put his hand with the fifty-five cents into hers, and said, "Take the money all back, Mom, and just let me love you and Dad and help you for nothing."

71

SOLOMON AND
THE BEES

Solomon was one of the greatest kings of the Jews. He was also one of the wisest men who ever lived.

Once the Queen of Sheba made a long journey to visit Solomon and to see if he was really wise. She brought him many beautiful presents and asked him many hard questions. Solomon answered every question correctly.

But one day the Queen thought of a
new way to test his wisdom. She invited
Solomon to come to a grand feast in the
palace garden. Then she said to him,
"King, among these flowers are some
that were made by skilled workmen. Tell
me, I pray you, which of the flowers are
real and which are not?"

Solomon looked at the flowers a long

time, but he could see no difference between them. But then he had an idea. He
turned to his servants and said, "Bring
in a hive of bees."

When the servants came back, the
King said, "Now put the bees down
among the flowers."

In a moment the bees began flying all
over the garden looking for honey. But

they flew only to the real flowers, for of course there was no honey in the man-made ones.

When the Queen of Sheba saw this, she bowed low before Solomon. "You are indeed a wise man, O King. You have answered my question."

"Not I," said Solomon smiling, "but my counselors the bees. Anything that is not real, O Queen, will give itself away sooner or later."

THANKSGIVING
IN REVERSE

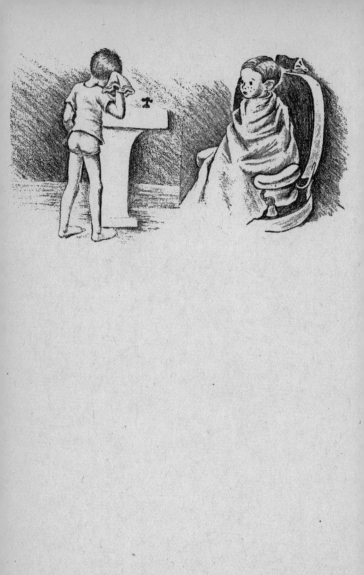

Dear God, You know all about me—even
my thoughts—
So I guess You know
there are some things I'm not thankful
for...
Things like having to wash so often,
especially behind my ears...
Getting my hair cut
and getting scratchy hair down my
neck...
Shots at the doctor's...
Having to go to bed so early
when exciting things are still happening

Waiting such a long time for grownups
when they say, "Presently, dear—"
Having to share my red wagon with that
new little boy . . .
The way my baby sister crawls on my
toys and bangs them around and yells
quite a lot . . .
Measles—and freckles and warts . . .
Flies and mosquitoes (Why did You
make them anyway?)
I guess grownups
always have things
they don't like either.

I guess it will always be that way;
But I'm just me
and I can't seem to make myself over.
So—dear God, since You made me in the
first place,
I'm sure You can change me.
Will you please help me
to stand the things I have to stand?
And help me to be nice to my baby sister
and the new little boy?
Thank You, God, for Your help.

                                    Amen

THE BOY WITH THE
SHINING FACE

In the Far West is an Indian village. Rising out of the desert and towering over the village is a high mountain. Only the very strong can climb it, so all the boys of the village were eager to try.

One day the chief said, "Now, boys, today you may try to climb the mountain. Each of you go as far as you can. When you are too tired to go on, come back. But I want each of you to bring me a twig from the place where you turned back."

Very soon a fat boy came puffing back. In his hand he held out to the chief a cactus leaf. The chief smiled. "My boy, you did not even reach the foot of the mountain. Cactus is a desert flower."

Later a second boy returned. He carried a twig of sagebrush. "Well," said the chief, "at least you reached the foot of the mountain."

The next boy to come back had in his hand a cottonwood twig. "Good," said the chief. "You climbed as far as the springs."

Another boy came back with some buckthorn. "You, my boy, were really climbing. You were up to the first slide rock."

An hour afterward, one boy came back with a branch of pine. To him the chief said, "Good! You made three-quarters of the climb."

The sun was low in the sky when the last boy returned. His hands were empty, but his face was shining. He said, "Father, there were no trees where I was. I saw no twigs, but I saw a shining sea."

Now the old chief's face glowed too. "I knew it! When I looked at your face, I knew it. . . . You have been to the top.

You needed no twig to tell me. It is written in your eyes. You alone, my boy, have seen the glory and the peace of the mountain."

You know, the very same thing happens to you and me when we have been with our Father in heaven and have talked to Him in prayer and felt His Presence in our hearts. It shows on our faces. It shines in our eyes. We don't have to tell anyone. Other people will see it and know and be glad.

FOLLOW THE LEADER

The Morris family had been on a picnic. As they got in their car to start home, Patty Morris asked, "What's that, Dad?" pointing to a swirling mist in the air.

"That's fog," her father answered. "And it's hard to drive in."

He drove very slowly, but could scarcely see through the fog enough to stay on the road. Suddenly another car, going much faster, passed him.

"That man seems to know where he's going," Mr. Morris said. "I think I'll just follow his red tail lights."

So they drove along that way for a while, until all at once the red tail lights ahead disappeared. Then—Wham! There was a loud crash. Patty was jolted a bit, but no one was hurt. This is what had happened. . . .

They had followed the man in the car ahead right into his own garage and had knocked his car smack through the back garage wall.

Mr. Morris stood looking at the splintered garage wall and the dented cars and said sadly, "Well, Patty, I guess it isn't safe to follow people unless you know where they are going."

He was right. There is really only one Leader whom you can safely follow, and that Leader is Jesus Christ. Let Him lead you, and everything will be all right.

I KNEW GOD WAS THERE

After my playing was over
I went into our house;
The fire was lit;
The kitchen smelled so nice—like ginger;
I knew my Mother was at home,
Even though I could not see her.

After my breakfast was over
I went outside to play;
The rugs of grass were laid;
The earth smelled so nice—like flowers;
I knew God was there,
Even though I could not see Him.

—ELIZABETH ANNE CAMPAGNA

THE LATCHSTRING WAS OUT

Long ago doors were fastened with a heavy wooden latch. The door could be opened from the outside by a thong made of deerskin. When this latch was pulled inside, no one could open the door. So friendly people used to say, "Come and see me soon. The latchstring is out." That meant that guests were welcome.

Once when the city of Cincinnati was just a frontier fort, the Indians went on the warpath. Most of the settlers grew frightened and rushed inside the fort for safety.

But there was one family that stayed on in its log cabin outside the fort. They had come from William Penn's colony in Pennsylvania and were called Friends or Quakers. William Penn had taught them that when the Indians were treated kindly, as God wants all men and women to be treated, they would be peaceful and friendly. Penn had proved that this was right, for back in Pennsylvania there were no Indian wars.

So the family in the cabin decided to try Penn's way. They did not even have any guns ready.

But one night the man grew a bit frightened and put the latchstring on the inside. He and his wife could not go to sleep. Finally she said, "John, that latchstring on the inside makes me feel uneasy."

"I feel that way too, Mary," he replied. So he got up and put the latchstring outside again.

Before long they heard the Indians coming. Soon they surrounded the little cabin with wild cries and war whoops.

They tried the door and saw that it would open, but did not come in. Then, after a while, they grew quiet and began to steal away. Mary and John crept on hands and knees to a window and watched them. On the edge of the forest, the Indians sat down in a circle. They seemed to be holding a council to talk things over.

"What do you suppose they're going to do?" Mary whispered.

"Sh-h-h," said John. "Remember God has promised us, 'I will never leave thee or forsake thee.'"

But soon they saw a tall chieftain in war paint leave the circle. Slowly he walked back to the cabin alone. In his right hand he carried a long white feather. He fastened the feather to the top of the cabin door. Then all the Indians left.

There the white feather stayed for a long time. The hot summer sun shone on it. It swayed in the winter winds that swept the prairie. John and Mary never took it down. For a friendly Indian told them: "The white feather means: 'This is the home of a man of peace. Do not harm him.'"

All this happened long ago. But God has not changed. He still wants us to be kind and fair to all men, and then to trust Him to take care of us.

PICTURE OF PEACE

There was once a king who offered a
prize to the artist who would paint the
best picture of peace. Many artists tried.
The king looked at all the pictures. But
there were only two that he really liked,
and he had to choose between them.

One picture was of a calm lake. The
lake was a perfect mirror for peaceful
towering mountains all around it. Over-
head was a blue sky with fluffy white
clouds. All who saw this picture thought
that it was a perfect picture of peace.

The other picture had mountains too.
But these were rugged and bare. Above
was an angry sky, from which rain fell
and in which lightning played. Down the

side of the mountain tumbled a foaming waterfall. This did not look peaceful at all.

But when the king looked closely, he saw behind the waterfall a tiny bush growing in a crack in the rock. In the bush a mother bird had built her nest. There, in the midst of the rush of angry water, in the wind and the noise, sat the mother bird on her nest—in perfect peace.

Which picture do you think won the prize? The king chose the second picture. Do you know why?

"Because," explained the king, "peace does not mean to be in a place where there is no noise, trouble, or hard work. Peace means to be in the midst of all those things and still be calm in your heart. That is the real meaning of peace."

HOW TO GET THE BEST OF A BURGLAR

Jesus told us to do some things which seem strange. For example, He said that when a man wants to take away our coat, we should not only let him have it and not fight back, but we should also give him our cloak (Matthew 5:40).

Why do you suppose Jesus said that? He was very wise. He knew that when

we fight back, we just make more
trouble for ourselves. But when we do
not fight back, then He can help us.

When something we say or do sur-
prises another person, we say they are
"dis-armed." Jesus' way is sometimes
really disarming.

I know a man who did exactly what
Jesus said. His name was Brother Bryan.
He was a minister who lived in Bir-
mingham, Alabama.

One Thursday night Brother Bryan
had stayed late at his church and was
walking home alone. As he crossed a
narrow, dark alley, a man stuck a gun
in his ribs and said, "Stick 'em up."

Brother Bryan obediently put up his
hands, and the thief searched through
his pockets and took his watch and some
money.

"Brother," said the minister, "you've
missed some. There's a little more money
in the other pocket." Then, as the thief
reached for that too, he was astonished
to hear his victim say, "Brother, let us
pray."

And the minister did pray. His prayer had a surprising effect. The thief hurriedly thrust all the money and the watch back into Brother Bryan's hands and rushed away without a single thing. Jesus' way had worked!

LITTLE DOG LOST

Dear Jesus, this is Johnny again . . .
My dog Jeff is lost, and I need Your help;
I had him for his evening walk;
He broke away to chase a squirrel—
Before I could catch him, he was out of sight,
Mums and Dad and I have searched everywhere . . .
And how can I enjoy my warm bed tonight with Jeffey in the cold?
(He can't chase squirrels all night!)
So, dear Jesus, will You please take care of Jeff and lead him safely home?
Thank You for this special help.

Amen

He prayeth best who loveth best
All things both great and small;
For the dear God who loveth us,
He made and loveth all.

—COLERIDGE

THE BIRDS'
CHRISTMAS TREE

It was Christmas Eve. Outside, the snow was falling in big downy flakes. When we picked up the evening paper from our front steps, we found it almost covered with snow. On the front page was this little notice:

ATTENTION: BIRD LOVERS

This is proving to be a hard winter for the birds in this area to find food. Why not remember the birds too at Christmastime?

I read the notice to Peter John. "I know!" he said excitedly. "Why can't we fix a Christmas tree for the birds?"

Peter-daddy and I agreed that this would be a fine idea.

"Let's put it on the porch of my birdhouse," Peter John said. This was a house he had made in shop at school. It was mounted on a pole in the back yard, and the whole family was proud of it.

We decorated the birds' tree with bits of colored yarn, some tiny popcorn balls, and some cranberries strung together. Then we tied things on the branches that the birds would like: small doughnuts; some empty walnut shells filled with

120

raisins, cracked corn, and sunflower seeds; others filled with peanut butter. We packed some soft suet into pine cones and fastened the cones to the tree.

Then we hid inside the house and watched out of the windows to see what would happen. In no time at all a blue jay, a chickadee, and three sparrows were enjoying a feast. Then came a song sparrow and a pair of redbirds. One of the redbirds stopped eating long enough to sit on top of the birdhouse and sing awhile. Since he was the right Christmas color, we thought he must surely be singing a bird's carol. Anyway, he seemed to be saying in his own way, "Thank you for remembering God's small creatures at Christmastime."

THE TOY DOG

"Hurry, Caspar." It was the eldest of the Wise Men of the East who spoke. "Why do you delay? The camels are ready; the way is long. We must get started."

But still Caspar—the youngest of the Wise Men—delayed. Rich gifts for the newborn Babe, the King of Kings, were already laden upon the patient camels—sacks filled with gold, frankincense, and myrrh. A brilliant star stood in a sapphire sky, waiting to point the way. But still Caspar lingered.

When the others asked him why he delayed, the young king could not tell. The camels, in their crimson and gold trappings, finally grew restless, and swayed and snarled. Purple shadows lengthened across the cooling sands of the desert. Still Caspar sat and thought deeply.

At length, he smiled and rose. Hurriedly, he mounted to a high-vaulted chamber at the top of his palace. This was the room in which he had played as a child. He rummaged about, and after a while came out, bearing something in his hand.

The Wise Men thought that Caspar surely bore some new gift, more rare and precious than all the riches they had been able to find in their treasure rooms. But in Caspar's hand was a toy. It was a cuddly dog, its soft white fur a little soiled.

Still smiling, the young king pressed his fingers to the dog's sides, and lo, it barked! A child, the son of one of the camel drivers, laughed and clapped his hands. But the older Wise Men looked stern and disapproving.

"What folly has seized you, Caspar?" cried the eldest. "Is that a gift fit for the King of Kings?"

But Caspar replied gently, "For the King of Kings, we have all these rare and costly treasures. But this—this toy dog—is a birthday gift for the Child of Bethlehem."

BIRTHDAY WISH

Jesus, when You were six like me,
Was six a lovely age to be?
And did You stand up straight and tall
For birthday measures on the wall?
Did You have candles on *Your* cake,
A special birthday wish to make?
Please bless all children on their Day
And make them happy in their play.

—ELIZABETH ANNE CAMPAGNA